A FUTURE WITH HOPE

**Aging creatively in
Christian community.**

A FUTURE WITH HOPE

Aging creatively in Christian community.

Harvey Kline
and
Warren Eshbach

THE BRETHREN PRESS
Elgin, Illinois

Cover design by Ken Stanley
Drawings by Cindy Staub

Library of Congress Cataloging in Publication Data

Eshbach, Warren M., 1940-
A future with hope.

Bibliography: p.
1. Old age. 2. Aged. 3. Church work with the
aged. I. Kline, Harvey S., 1921-   joint author.
II. Title.
HV1451.E84   261.8'34'35   78-17720
ISBN O-87178-298-7

We need hope for living, far more than for dying. Dying is easy work, compared to living. Dying is a moment's transition; living, a transaction of years. It is the length of the rope that puts the sag in it. Hope tightens the words and tunes up the heartstrings.
                                                    —Telescope-Messenger

CONTENTS

FOREWORD

It has been said that the quality of a society can be determined by the manner in which it responds to the needs of its children and its elderly. For a long time, the church has placed much emphasis upon children and youth. We have seen, as a result, intensified youth programming and a higher level of participation by younger people in the life of the church.

A new focus, however, has developed as the church has begun to give increasing attention to those at the other end of the life cycle. The result has been new understandings of the process of aging and the development of more creative ministries for the older person. If we are to minister effectively to the aging, it is important that we understand the particular aspects of need and change which are experienced by persons who are at the latter end of the life cycle. We need to recognize the unique contribution that can be made by older persons, the enrichment they offer to an understanding of our heritage, the values of increased inter-generational relationships, and the opportunity the church has to offer a dynamic and creative ministry for and with senior citizens.

Ministry to older people takes place basically at the local level (only five per cent of persons over sixty-five are in institutional settings). The church has an opportunity to join with community groups, with social services agencies, and with the retirement/nursing homes in offering a program of intentional ministry for all older persons. It is a pleasure to be able to commend this book written by two persons who write out of both knowledge and experience. Harvey S. Kline and Warren M. Eshbach both have a theological background, pastoral experience and practical involvement in gerontological ministry. It is hoped their writing will stimulate you to further reading as you seek to be better equipped to understand your own aging process and to relate to others around you.

J. Stanley Earhart
District Executive
Southern Pennsylvania
Church of the Brethren

Age is a quality of mind;
If you've left your
Dreams behind,
If hope is cold,
If you no longer look ahead,
If your ambitious fires
Are dead,
Then, you are old!
    —Anonymous

I grow old learning something new every day. —Solon (638?-559 B.C.)

1
WHAT IT MEANS
TO GROW OLDER

Life is a cycle which continues to turn, change, and grow. Like the snowballs you made as a child which grew larger and thicker with each layer of snow as you rolled them along, our lives grow fuller and more abundant as we grow older.

Do you realize that you are older now than at the time you woke up this morning? Are you aware that you have aged since you acquired this book? The writer of Ecclesiastes affirmed what he recognized in his own life and life around him when he wrote,

> For everything there is a season . . .
> A time to be born and a time to die.
> (Eccl. 3:1-2)

Between the time we are born and the time we die our life is engaged in a process of growth and fulfillment. From the cries of infancy, through the growing pains of adolescence, to the rigidity of the middle years, we progress toward the fulfillment of our lives. For many people this growth is creative and full of rich experiences; for many more, "growing older" means fear of illness and a sense of unfulfilled dreams and aspirations.

One of the lamentable tendencies of our society is that younger people tend often to see an aging person as an "it" or "them," rather than recognizing that older people are "us." We are all going to be old some day, and a perspective on the process of aging, caught at an early age, will enhance one's understanding and acceptance of every individual.

Growing older is to recognize change in yourself and discover ways and methods to adapt to that change as well as changes within the world around you. Persons who have that ability are cognizant of their own aging, and with the aid of their Christian faith they accept both the joys and sorrows of the aging process in an understanding and creative way.

As you read this book, take a serious look at the Scriptures, yourself, and those around you to affirm that every stage of life can be on "the growing edge."

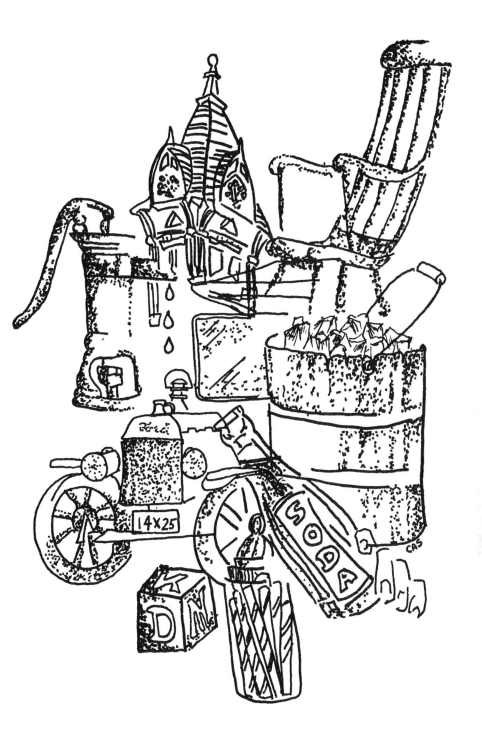

Every age has its pleasure, its style of wit, and its own ways. —Nicholas Boileau-Despréaux (1636-1711)

2
PREMISES FOR CONSIDERING THE AGING PROCESS

In speaking to the 1970 White House Conference on Aging, Jewish writer Abraham Heschel concluded in this cryptic way:

> Old men need a vision, not only recreation.
> Old men need a dream, not only a memory.
> It takes three things to attain a sense of significant being:
> (1) God
> (2) A Soul
> (3) And a moment.
> And the three are always here.
> Just to be is a blessing. Just to live is holy.

It is our fundamental assumption that the church needs to be concerned with aging people, and not only with aging people, but the aging process itself. Because growing older is something that happens to everyone and because the number and percentage of persons in our society who are over 65 are increasing, it is imperative that the church give its attention to this basic human reality.

The ideas we hope to inspire the church to consider as it addresses itself to the aging process can be grouped under six key words: ministry, universality, minority, normalcy, diversity, and family.

1. *Ministry.* Anything affecting human life comes within the purview of the church's concern and ministry. It is the role of the church to be seeking always to enrich and nurture our lives. Our concern is that the church historically has failed to emphasize the importance of the aging process, and particularly as the aging process affects older people. Consequently, the dropout rate for participation in church functions by older people is frequently very high. This neglect on the part of the church has not been so much deliberate as it has been insensitivity to the needs of older people. For example, it is only in the most recent years that church architecture has taken into account the need to make the facilities of the building accessible to aged and handicapped people. How many church buildings do you know in which you can enter the sanctuary and the church school area without climbing steps? How much attention does the average congregation give to providing transportation for senior citizens? To be sure, the church is not only its activities and its building, but these are important phases of the everyday ministry that the church provides in our lives.

Across the years the church has embraced special emphases such as youth and family life. While these are also vital ministries, it is astounding that so little has been said, until recent times, about the aging process, particularly since all of us are involved in it.

2. *Universality.* Aging is not just something that happens to someone else. It is not something that happens only to people of advanced years. Aging is something in which all of us are engaged. We age chronologically by the calendar, we age biologically by the condition of our bodies, and we age psychologically by the ways in which we act and feel. To put it in other words, we are aging from the moment of conception until death.

3. *Minority.* "Minority" is a popular term in our day. When we talk about older people, we are in essence talking about the largest minority in our society. There are today some 21 million people in the United States over the age of 65, with the ratio of men and women 65 and older, 143 women to 100 men. Four thousand people in the United States reach 65 daily and three thousand people above the age of 65 die each day. This makes a net increase of those in our society over 65 of 1,000 each day. The group from 75 to 85 is among the most rapidly growing minorities.

The number of people age 65 and older has grown in the past 20 years from 12 million to 21 million, and by 1985 it is expected to reach 26 million people. Some students of the future have indicated that by 1985 promotional/marketing programs which explicitly advertise the over-65 factor will indeed be counterproductive.

The following graph points out the growing need for the church to be concerned and involved.

1850, 65+ were 2.5% of U.S. population
1900, 65+ were 4% of U.S. population
1950, 65+ were 8% of U.S. population
1975, 65+ were 10.4% of U.S. population
2000, 65+ will be 33% of U.S. population, according to a projection reported by Sylvia Porter.

It is estimated that the deaths of as many as 75% of the people occur in a hospital or nursing home. The fact that in some cases they die alone is an additional concern in the church's ministry to older people.

Yet another statistic is significant: it has been estimated by some that as many as one-third of the people living today over the age of 65 have a living aged parent. What a tremendous opportunity this suggests to the church for education in inter-generational relationships.

4. *Normalcy.* To age is normal. Aging is a process and not a disease nor a peculiarity. Aging is very individualized, to be sure, but it is universal in that it affects all of us! Yet, in spite of the inevitability of aging in human life, 87% of 101 United States medical schools surveyed by a Senate sub-committee on long-term care have no specialized program in geriatric medicine nor plans to institute such a program. There appears then to be a long way to go in the recognition that aging is normal and requires attention!

A basic question is: Do we face this issue from the viewpoint of geriatrics or gerontology? If we face it from the point of view of geriatrics, it is easy to dismiss the whole question of the aging process because it is restricted to a study of diseases of aging people. However there are no diseases that are exclusively associated with old age, for what affects older people has also been found to affect persons of every age group.

On the other hand, if we look at it from the viewpoint of gerontology then we come to see that all of us are involved, for gerontology is a study of the aging process, a process active within us from the moment of our conception to the time of our death.

We are talking, therefore, about the element of choice. In one of Noel Coward's plays two of his characters reflect in this serious conversation. The lady is saying, "I think life is for living. Don't you?" After a long pause, her male companion replies, "It's hard to know what else you'd do with it." This sets it forth quite well! The church in recognizing the normalcy of aging should be concerned not only with the quantity but with the quality of the earthly years.

5. *Diversity.* Maybe one of the reasons we have neglected to talk about or to concern ourselves with the aging process is because of the diversity of aging's effects. One can go to a textbook and discover some of the average characteristics of a six-year-old or a twelve-year-old but one can scarcely do the same for a person who is 65, 75 or 85.

One explanation for the differences in the aging process may well be related to the diverse ways in which people look at themselves. One writer has observed that some people of older years act in a peculiar way because this is the way they believe society expects older people to act. Scientific study has indicated that senility is not automatic with old age, but rather that for many people senility is actually their choice. Autopsies performed on people of older age have revealed that there were persons who passed away *with* brain damage but who were *not* senile, and some people who had *no* brain damage but who *were* senile. The conclusion seems to be that senility in some significant measure is a matter of our own choosing.

The potential problem of senility is compounded because medical opinion may wrongly diagnose an elderly person as senile when proper understanding of the symptoms and proper treatment may actually effect a cure for the "senility." To have a doctor think of his patient first as "old" and secondly as a "person" is really to reverse the proper order! An older person is a person who happens to be of advanced years!

In addition, most of us know "senile" persons who are playing the role their environment expects of them. Both family and church can help to produce senile responses in older members of the community. It is only by conscious effort that this unfortunate expectation can be eliminated. People should be allowed to be themselves, whether twenty or ninety years of age!

Learning can take place as long as a person lives. As a matter of fact, learning is one of the essential ingredients to good life. When learning ceases, then life is no more than existence. While the pace may be slower for a person of 85 than for a person of 12 each is able to learn. The brain cells are kept active by being used, and conversely, they deteriorate by disuse.

A professional magazine in the field of aging carried a report of a woman, 87, who was worrying about her mother who was 107 and living in a nursing home. However, she had some help because she had a sister aged 83.

Another example of active and productive longevity is an 85-year-old man who was delivering hot meals on his birthday with this explanation, "I want to help older people."

On the other hand, a 92-year-old attorney, resident of a nursing home, when asked how he was faring replied with negative and disdainful feeling. "To think it comes to this," he sighed.

These simple illustrations are not intended to minimize the realistic problems of growing older, but to indicate that a positive acceptance and attitude toward the later years will help make them productive rather than bitter.

On the question of longevity, there seems to be a consensus that the purpose of the medical and scientific studies today are not so much to actually lengthen the span of life beyond about 90 years, but to slow down "the pace of aging." Life expectancy today is usually regarded as something over 66 years for men and 74 years for women. However, in reality when a woman is age 74 she can expect another 10 years of life. When people are 65, they can normally look forward to about 15 additional years of life. These averages say something about our pattern of expectation. Life expectancy increases as one achieves the additional plateau of years.

6. *Family.* Because more people are achieving the distinction of living more than 65 years; because this represents also an increase in the percentage of our total population; and because the retirement age is now considered to be 70; the experiences of those in this retirement category affect the lives of the family, the church, and the community.

A time line reflecting three phases of life can be used to work through feeling concerning aging—your own and that of parents or other family members. Phase one is the first 20 years of life; phase two, ages

20-50; and phase three, the 50+ span.

The first 20 years represent distinctive roles in parent-child relationships. The parent is the protector and the provider, and the child may accept or may rebel, but he is always subject to the authority of the parent. In the second phase, the child has achieved independent adulthood and may have entered a marriage relationship of his or her own. The two families, while communicating, are nevertheless two separate entities and express this in terms of decision making. In the third phase, however, the aging parent may well become increasingly dependent upon the child. The demand now is for the child to make choices for the well-being of the parent. In effect, this makes one her/his parents' parent. With no advance preparation for this change in role for both parent and child, the emotional and intellectual cost may be high. Some families make this transition smoothly but in too many families, where the process is not understood, there is frequently much dissension and friction.

Recognizing the wide range of effects the aging process can have upon individuals, families, and communities, it is our basic assumption that the church needs to play an increasing role in helping its membership creatively face the issue of life's unfolding phases. The time has now come when the church must help the largest minority in her membership achieve the "good life" at the crowning point of life's ladder. We begin this process not so much by technique as by a basic attitude or posture. Just to seek to understand and then to determine to be involved creatively are two of the fundamental stepping stones upon which we invite you to begin.

To look upon the soul as going on from strength to strength, to consider that it is to shine forever with new accessions of glory, and brighten to all eternity; that it will be still adding virtue to virtue, and knowledge to knowledge—carries in it something wonderfully agreeable to that ambition which is natural to the mind of men.
—Joseph Addison (1672-1719)

The short period of life is long enough for living well and honourably.—Cicero (106-43 B.C.)

3
THE BIBLICAL VIEW
OF AGING

An outstanding trait in the primitive cultures of world civilization was their ability to honor and respect the aging person of society. Unlike our modern world where vast sums of money are spent on advertising to promote youthfulness, earlier cultures revered the aged person as someone with skill, wisdom, and discernment.

Christian persons who take their Judeo-Christian heritage seriously soon discover that the biblical attitude toward the older person is a far cry from what they experience in American and Western society today. What are the ideas about the process of aging in

the Old and New Testaments? How can these basic
ideas be valuable tools in helping us become liberated
from the awesome fear of growing old?

In ancient Israel the strongest social unit was
that of the tribal family. Within each family was the
zaqen, or elder, who was in the highest position of
respect. The elder, literally a term meaning "full
beard," was the person of the household who because
of age was given the authority to rule and make
decisions for the family. As the tribal family evolved
as a major social force in ancient Israel, it soon made
its influence felt in the community at large. Here the
zaqen or elders of more powerful families exerted an
influence over the social and economic decisions of
the town or city. They would assemble themselves in
session at the gate of the town and render judgments
on the important and weighty matters of the day.
Ruth 4:2 ff. gives an example of the kinds of issues in
which the elders were involved. In that story they
help to consummate the plans for the marriage vows
for Ruth and Boaz. The elders were the judges, advisors, and administrators of the social institutions of
early Israel. They were esteemed in the political struc-
ture because they were "old."

During the days of the monarchy, the eldership
was solidified to the point where every house in town
was governed by these old advisors who knew the
Law and were acquainted with divine wisdom
through the experience of living. To the Israelite people, wisdom was not intellectual education alone, but
was experiential in nature. This meant that understanding and wisdom were attained through long life.
It was to the elders of long life that the monarchy
gave the responsibility for making decisions "at the
gate." It even used these men in its own court as ad-

visors to the king.

It is interesting to note that in 1 Kings 12:6 ff. the blame for the division of the United Kingdom is laid at the feet of King Rehoboam because "he rejected the advice which the elders had given him, and spoke to the people as the young men had advised." (1 Kings 12:13-14, NEB)

Ancient Israel gave great credit to the older person as evidenced by the veneration age receives throughout the Old Testament writings. The old person was honored by the Torah or the Law. It is in the decalogue where this principle is prominently displayed:

> Honor your father and your mother, that your days may be long in the land which the Lord your God gives you. (Exodus 20:12, RSV)

Here the idea is advanced that God is calling his people to honor their parents because it was through them that God's breath of life had been transmitted to the children. A long and fulfilled life was promised if this principle was followed. Proverbs 3:1-2 infers that by keeping the Commandments, "long life, years in plenty, and peace will be added to thee."

Apart from seeing the aging process as directly connected with learning the Torah or the Law, Israel also believed that old age was synonymous with wisdom. People in the society were instructed to honor the aging. Proverbs 20:29 states:

> The glory of young men is their strength, but the beauty of old men is their grey hair. (RSV)

From the above examples it is clear that the social *mores* of ancient Israel placed a premium on old age and considered being old as not only prestigious, but desirable as well. The Scriptures also

reveal that unexpected events could take place in old
age because God's hand was a part of the growing
process with all of its pains and pleasures. One such
example is the story of Sarah and the birth of Isaac
in Genesis 18:12 ff. At the very time when Sarah
believes it impossible to give birth because the aging
process has affected the sexual vitality of both her
and her husband, God reveals his covenantal promise
that Isaac shall be born.

But the aging process is not always a beautiful or
an exciting experience. For many it is marked by suffering and ill health. The biblical writers recognize
the realities of failing health in old age and speak
forthrightly about it. We discover that Abraham "had
become a very old man" (Genesis 24:1) and in recognizing this, the "father of the faith" sought to make
provisions for his son Isaac to marry and carry on
the heritage of God's promise. Abraham, sensing the
finality of his old age, realistically faced his own impending death. In so doing, he could make
preparations for his son.

We discover that the failing eyesight of Isaac was
the reason that the birthright scuffle between Esau
and Jacob could actually go unnoticed. Perhaps this
was the first example of trickery used on older
members of the family—a practice which still goes on
today. It is interesting to note that Jacob in his later
years also suffered from blindness as did his father.
(Genesis 48:10)

While the maladies of old age are recognized
throughout the scriptures, none became quite so vivid
as those portrayed by some of the psalm writers of
Israel. Psalm 31 is a lament written by a person who
has experienced suffering for many years. The words
leap out of the Scriptures and become reality for

many older persons today who can identify with the depth of the psalmist's lament:

> My eyes are tired from so much crying;
> I am completely worn out!
> I am exhausted by sorrow,
> And weeping has shortened my years.
> I am weak from all my troubles,
> even my bones are wasting away.
>   (Psalm 31:9-10, TEV)

As if the condition of this person were not pitiful enough, it becomes even more pathetic when the issue of loneliness is introduced. Here the psalmist pours out the depths of human suffering which are always aggravated by the wretchedness of isolation:

> Everyone has forgotten me, as though I were dead;
> I am like something thrown away.
>   (Psalm 31:12, TEV)

Thus the plight of many sick and elderly persons is identified. This condition affects even the life of the faithful and is stated again in another lament from Psalm 38 where the sick person gives the view of one suffering from a condition that leaves him bent over and troubled with ailments of the heart:

> If I am bent over, I am crushed;
> I mourn all day long.
> I am burning with fever and I am near death.
> I am worn out and utterly crushed; my heart is troubled and I groan with pain.
> My friends and neighbors will not come near me because of my sores;
> even my family stays away from me.
>   (Psalm 38:6-8, 11, TEV)

These scriptures help us understand that old age
has its troublesome times as well as its periods of
freedom and creativity.

Perhaps one of the most interesting stories in the
Bible concerning the persistence of ill health in old
age is found in 1 Kings 1:1-4. This passage describes
how King David suffered continually from being cold.
To this day, old persons can attest to this aggrava-
tion even on warm days. To remedy the situation, the
king of Israel had a young and beautiful maiden put
in his bed with him. She was there for no other purpose than to keep him warm.

Though such a remedy as this would have moral
implications and overtones if it were tried today, the
account does relate how the king's servants sought to
deal with David's arteriosclerosis.

In each of the examples cited above, it is clear
that the Old Testament writers did not seek to hide
the hard realities of health that beset the elderly. Old
age was the result of righteous living (Psalm 92:14),
and the God of steadfast love would give strength to
those who suffered.

Though many in society today would shun the
elderly and lock them out of hopes, aspirations, and
dreams, certain of the Messianic passages in the Old
Testament give special prominence to the role of older men and women in the new Kingdom. When
the prophet Joel speaks about the outpouring
of the Spirit, he proclaims the word of the Lord as
saying:

> I will pour out my Spirit on all mankind.
> Your sons and daughters shall prophesy
> and your old men will dream dreams.
> (Joel 2:28, Jerusalem Bible)

Zechariah also gives a special place to the elevation of "old men and old women" in the Messianic kingdom. But significant is the fact that along with them will be boys and girls, a clear reference to the fact that in the Kingdom the generations should learn from each other and show respect toward the place of each:

> Yahweh Sabbaoth says this
> Old men and old women will again sit down in the squares of Jerusalem; every one of them staff in hand because of their great age.
> And the squares of the city will be full of boys and girls playing in the square.
> (Zechariah 8:4-5, Jerusalem Bible)

The Old Testament reflects how the society of Israel revered and held a place for its elders *zaqen*. At the same time, it illustrates how the aging process can be one of struggle as well. But always beyond the suffering is the God of steadfast love, who promises restoration and peace in the new Kingdom that is to come.

When the Christ event occurs, the concept of the wisdom of the elderly has a prominent place in the personages of Simeon and Anna. As the Kingdom of God silently breaks through to the world in the infant son of Mary and Joseph, it is at the dedication in the temple where an old man with wisdom and warmth grasps the reality of what God is doing in the affairs of his people:

> Now in Jerusalem there was a man named Simeon. He was an upright and devout man; he looked forward to Israel's comforting and the Holy Spirit rested on him . . . It had been revealed to him by the Holy Spirit that he would not see

death until he had set eyes on the Christ of the
Lord. Prompted by the Spirit, he came to the Temple; and when the parents brought in the child
Jesus to do for him what the Law required, he
took him into his arms and blessed God; and he
said:

'Now, Master, you can let your servant go in
peace, just as you promised; because my eyes
have seen the salvation which you have prepared
for all the nations to see; a light to enlighten the
pagans and the glory of your people Israel.'
                              (Luke 2:25-32, Jerusalem Bible)

Like Simeon, Anna, who is an old prophetess,
also recognizes the glory and salvation of God in the
child, Jesus. Through the smile of an old man and the
praise of an old woman, the world comes to see more
clearly the glory of God which breaks into the lives of
all people. What was true centuries ago can be realized today, if we take time to listen and comprehend
what the elderly of our time have to say about life
and deliverance.

The concept of the elder which is prevalent in the
Old Testament is also carried over into the New. Here
the word *presbuteros* has the same basic understanding as *zaqen*. It means "aged person."

In Matthew 15:2 ff. Jesus makes a very subtle
reference to revering and honoring the older persons
of society when he chastises the Pharisees for not doing "duty to father and mother." Jesus makes
reference to this when the Pharisees accused his disciples of "breaking the tradition of the elders"
because they did not wash their hands before eating.
Jesus immediately turns the situation around and
reminds the Pharisees that they are not honoring
their fathers and mothers because they are using the

money in the temple rather than utilizing it to care for their parents.

Once more the idea of respect for the older person is made quite clear. The question of caring for the mother and father is a real one in our present day society. While some such as the Pharisees of old find excuses for neglecting this ministry, others discover real joy and meaning in caring for older persons, and in recognizing that we are all in the process of aging.

The thought of Jesus' day also reflects that aging is a process and that God's redemptive love can break in on that process at any age. When the angel speaks to Mary about her cousin Elizabeth who "has in her old age conceived a son" the implication is clear that to be old is not shameful or degrading but a part of life in which God can still work, and in that life process with God "nothing is impossible."

Old age is for many persons a time of decision making and struggle. One of the most difficult facts of life to accept is that of being dependent upon someone else. It is interesting that Jesus is aware of this emotion and seeks to comfort the apostle Peter by saying:

> When you were young you put on your own belt
> and walked where you liked; but when you grow
> old you will stretch out your hands and somebody
> else will put a belt around you and take you where
> you would rather not go.
>   (John 21:18, Jerusalem Bible)

In these words, Peter's death is not only foretold, but a reality of what it means to be old is also indicated. Many have discovered that these words of the Lord to Peter have become realities in life. For in old age, being "cared for" often involves residing at a place not of your choosing.

Our culture seems determined to deny the aging process while isolating those who are living through old age. What hope is there? The hope offered by the apostle Paul and affirmed by the whole biblical tradition suggests that persons recognize life in God's hand as a growing and maturing process and that while our physical bodies should be maintained, they are neither immortal nor of prime importance. For to comprehend the aging process in one's life an individual must recognize that the inner self or the heart, which in the Bible is the seat of the emotions, needs to be nurtured for living through each life cycle.

Writing in order to encourage the Church of Corinth, which was struggling against acculturation from Hellenism, Paul says:

> So we do not lose heart. Though our outer nature is wasting away, our inner nature is being renewed every day.
> (2 Corinthians 4:16-18, RSV)

This is one of the New Testament's greatest affirmations of the life cycle principle and the fact that no person can live forever in earthly time and space. As children of God, we are part of the created order which passes from the earthly scene. As disciples of Christ and citizens of his Kingdom, our hope for meaningful life rests in the fulfillment of the Kingdom and the inner renewal which takes place in our spirits as we pass through this life. To be aware of one's self in the aging process is to realize that we are "growing into the fullness of the stature of Christ" (Eph. 4:13). To grow this way is to confront aging with confidence and strength in the Christ who calls us to full maturity in him.

From this biblical survey of the aging process, we recognize the following things about the principle of aging:

(1) Old age is a reality of life and given honor in the Law or Torah.

(2) The term "elder" is always held in high esteem in the Old Testament, a tradition which is carried through into the New Testament Church.

(3) To be old is a sign of wisdom and strength.

(4) Infirmities can accompany old age.

(5) Persons who know Jesus as Lord understand aging to be a process which does not depend on the outer body, but on the renewal of the inner life in Christ.

I'm growing wise; I'm growing—yes,—I'm growing old!—
John Godfrey Saxe (1816-1887)

4

ADAPTING TO CHANGE

Who has not heard the statement "You cannot teach an old dog new tricks"? One might have real doubts about the maxim's accuracy, however. In fact, scientific studies have indicated that people of older years can continue to learn, if they so choose. To be sure, the pace at which the learning takes place may be slower than for a youthful person. The value of continued learning is to add meaning to each day and also to push back, or postpone, the probability of senility.

Scientists indicate to us that the brain cells of our body deteriorate differently from other body cells. The brain cells deteriorate by disuse whereas our other body cells are subject to evolutionary processes. Fortunate, therefore, is the person who sees each day as an opportunity for additional learning experiences!

It has also been said that older people are increasingly set in their ways! But the opposite viewpoint has been reported by a pastor sharing his parish experiences and having these experiences confirmed in conversation with other pastors. He noted that it is not really the older people of the parish who present the most resistance to growth and to change. It is the middle-aged members! The theory becomes more credible if we think in terms of priorities. He reminds us that young people are in the process of discovering their priorities and, therefore, are always in a state of change and flux. The older people, he contends, are consistently rediscovering and re-evaluating their priorities with a high degree of selectivity in their choices. Middle-aged people, however, are still actively defending their priorities and are defensive in the face of new ideas. This observation from pastors, who spend the majority of their time relating to people, suggests that the stereotyping of older people as static and unyielding is a generality quite unfounded.

Philadelphia based Grey Panther leader Maggie Kuhn advises, "Make old age the time of triumph, hope, strength, and joy; it is a time to reach out with love and with the time at our disposal to build a new community."

In view of such observations, it is truly remarkable how adaptable people of senior years are and, in fact, need to be in reacting to the challenges of daily living. We shall indicate a number of areas which reflect on the experiences of people of advanced years and which, by their very nature, require a considerable amount of adaptability, even if the goal is simply to survive. When one adds the dimension of meaning to survival, the adaptability of many people of advanced years is truly remarkable!

The startling rapidity with which technology is developing heightens the challenge to adapt. The generations of technology are now shorter than the generations of humankind. Numerous major adjustments are required within one's lifetime; for example, the average worker may need to be retrained four or five times during his productive years to remain abreast of new developments in his job.

As the pilgrimage through life approaches the advanced years one of the first major adjustments is the period called the "empty nest." This is the time when children have left home and the father and mother now need to re-emphasize their husband/wife roles. It is not without significance that the divorce rate jumps again at this point of marital life. How fortunate it is when a husband and a wife throughout the years have combined their parental roles with their marital relationships to each other. How unfortunate it is for the husband and wife who have assumed only their father/mother roles as their children were growing up and then come to this stage of life to discover that they are now living as comparative strangers.

This is the time also when menopause is most likely to occur; this often compounds feelings of uselessness. It is commonly thought that "the menopause" effects only women, but there is now evidence that many men experience a similar period of adjustment in their life cycle. For some people this is viewed as the beginning of the decline of life. Women sometimes assume that because they have lost their reproductive ability, they have also lost their physical attractiveness to their husbands. Husbands see this as a time in which they are no longer able to do some of the things they had done formerly because their strength is not equal to that of their younger days. Because their powers of recuperation are slowed, they too feel that they are in a decline of life. It can be helpful at this point if we see this as a part of life's unfolding and not as an entity in itself.

The role of grandparenthood requires another definite adaptation for older life. Proverbs 17:6 observes "grandchildren are the crown of the aged." This phase of life provides for some of the joys of sharing childhood without the same responsibility that parenthood entails. It may well serve to solidify the family to see this as a part of the continuity of the particular family lineage and humankind in general. Certainly, one of the very valuable contributions that grandparents can bring to grandchildren happens through the sharing of their time and their experiences. However, grandparents continually need to keep in mind that they are not the parents of the grandchildren, and remember therefore that the roles of responsibility are different. There are moments when this can be accepted with abiding joy and there are also moments when it can be deeply frustrating. The point is that this is an experience requiring a remarkable degree of adaptability on the part of the older generation. Many people have attested to the wonder and glory of the role of being a grandparent!

For some persons the joys of being a grandparent have helped to make retirement years more meaningful. The sudden relinquishing of a job to which one has routinely devoted the majority of his life is often a traumatic experience. A mid-nineteenth century ruler arbitrarily picked "age 65" as the magic age for retirement; the Social Security system of the mid 1930's in this country re-emphasized this "magic age" for the American' society, and only recently Congress extended retirement age to 70.

Retirement has some profound implications for us in that some people look forward to it eagerly and some people dread its coming. Some industries require it and thus throw away expert talent while other industries are now coming to recognize values in not having an arbitrary age at which retirement is required. Retirement definitely causes a time of readjustment. No longer does the man or the woman need to get up in the morning and then go off to his/her work. No longer is a time card waiting to be punched or an appointment demanding to be met! This change has important psychological implications. A person who has been accustomed to people coming to him because of his position discovers that people come less and less, and soon may not come at all to see him.

In our society, a man's self-esteem is peculiarly attached to his vocational position in life. Reflect a moment upon how you introduce someone. Do you not often do it in terms of the job that person holds? When that person is retired, then this description, at best, is that of an "ex."

The sudden increase in leisure, or personal choice time, that a retiree now has available requires special adaptability. For people who have not planned ahead, this can become burdensome and even death-producing. How many people do you know who have lived but a few years beyond retirement? It would appear that we are not created to be devoid of meaning and happenings.

Raymond R. Peters, former executive secretary of
the Church of the Brethren Annual Conference
Health and Welfare Committee, reports a survey in
which the question was asked of the general population, "What do you desire most in retirement?" The
response was, "Freedom from responsibility."
However, when that same question was directed to
people in the retirement years themselves, they made
a very significant distinction in saying that they
desired freedom from " . . . *some* responsibilities," i.e.
not *all*. All of us have a need to feel needed!

The adjustment to retirement is often compounded by a reduction in income, which vitally
affects one's standard of living in current American
society. A Pennsylvania study reveals that, on the
average, actual income in retirement years is reduced
by about one-half while many people in retirement
years feel that they need an income at about two-
thirds of their former level. Obviously, this creates
some financial stress.

The relationship between a husband and a wife
needs to be at a very satisfying level for couples to
make this adjustment. Those who have been able to
do it satisfactorily have shown a remarkable degree
of adaptability.

There is another dimension to retirement which
is not very often considered; that is the spouse's role.
First, let us consider the couple in which the husband
has been the "breadwinner" while the wife had
adopted or accepted the role of homemaker through
much of their married life. His retirement will be a
major adjustment in schedule and activity for him
while her life may change very little.

In such situations the wife usually needs to be

sympathetic and understanding of the profound changes which take place in her husband's life when he retires, particularly if he is forced to do so because he has now arrived at the "magic age" of 70. Many husbands may not be accustomed or willing to share in the domestic chores. On the other hand, some wives may resent the sudden intrusion upon their daytime sovereignty of the house. As one wife observed: "I know I married my husband for better or worse, but I did not marry him for lunch!" To make the retirement years meaningful requires a unique sensitivity on the part of both husband and wife to one another's needs and adjustment.

Since in today's society an increasing number of wives are gainfully employed, it would not be adequate to leave this discussion with the focus primarily upon the husband. Both husband and wife need to carefully and intentionally review together the meaning of retirement when they have both been gainfully employed. Retirement for these couples may not come at precisely the same time because of an age differential. One may be retired first with a large block of time available. This will call for some individual adjustment and it will also call for understanding on the part of the mate who is still actively involved in the employment world. This is a relatively new phenomenon and calls for the concern of both the church and the family in creatively meeting this new challenge. To include this in the educational approach of the family and the church is both wise and essential.

With longevity increasing, it is becoming more urgent for the church to provide a ministry to people of advanced years. As we have noted, when people have arrived at the age of 65, statistics show they can expect, on the average, approximately fifteen more years of life. Viewed with that prospect, approximately twenty percent of one's life is still ahead at age 65, much of which could still be spent in productive service to church, community, and family.

There is yet another area of adaptability which is frequently overlooked. This is the kind of adjustment which is needed by a person who faces either lingering or chronic illness. We have been told by the medical profession that many of the organs of the body are designed to live for a limited number of years and that the matter of transplanting is becoming popular to extend the functional life of the body.

Illness for an older person obviously is more serious than it is for a younger person, if for no other reason than that the recovery rate is slowed, sometimes considerably. A very active 70-year-old was reflecting upon his experience of the previous day on which his dentist had extracted one of his teeth. The dental practitioner had assured his patient that he would " . . . soon be over it and the effect (would be) minimal." "But," observed the aging gentleman, "when one is 70 it is not quite as minimal as when one is younger!"

How fortunate we are to be living in a society which gives increasingly more attention to the understanding and education for the onset of advanced age. Modern day medication is able to do things that were unknown before. While illness remains a problem, its seriousness is often offset by the aid which can come from an understanding physician who wisely combines counsel with medication.

We have yet to discuss two additional areas requiring adaptability. The first one is the more difficult; that is the death of a spouse. An administrator of a home for aging people recalls a conversation with a couple who were 90 years of age concerning their desire to become residents of the home. At the time of the interview, it appeared as though there would be space immediately for just the husband. The wife would need to wait until a vacancy in the home occurred. Even though it, fortunately, worked out that they entered the home together, the wife would say over and over, " . . . but we have always been together." She was reflecting on the fact that they had lived together as husband and wife for 65 years.

A pastor of a midwestern community told of a conversation with a very respected and faithful deacon who was in his seventies and had been widowed twice. He was a remarkable man in that he carried on a full life. He had learned to cook after he had retired and was able to prepare a delectable meal with "all the trimmings"! One day he remarked to his young pastor about "feeling alone in the world." He was referring, of course, to the death of his wife, but his pastor admitted having difficulty understanding what he meant because the pastor saw a neighborhood filled with friends and a church filled with concerned members. The scriptural admonition that "a man shall leave his father and mother and cleave unto his wife and they shall become one flesh," takes on very deep meaning when this principle has been lived across the years and then there is separation by the death of either husband or wife.

It is entirely proper and necessary to provide the opportunity for the surviving spouse to reflect back across the years of experience and to find fulfillment in memories to enhance the living of the present day. Obviously, the abrupt shift of the life pattern through the loss of a spouse requires a very large measure of adaptability.

A similar adjustment comes with the death of friends and other relatives. How many of us have heard older people indicate that they are the only ones left from their circle of friends or of their family? Frequently they talk of this with some degree of longing. We may have an important role in helping older people by permitting them to talk about the meaning of death and how the loss of their friends has affected them. Death is not a morbid experience for many older people as they talk about the future. This is particularly true for people with a strong Christian faith.

When grace is joined with wrinkles, it is adorable. There is an unspeakable dawn in happy old age.—Victor Hugo (1802-1885)

5
EXPOSING MYTHS ABOUT AGING

We are working on the premise that it is better to be informed than to accept ideas and notions which are not based on fact. There are many current ideas about aging which are either partially or entirely false. We propose to examine a number of commonly accepted myths about aging with the hope of discovering truths which will both improve our relationships with older people and help us more accurately assess our own aging patterns.

A popular publication indicates that the stereotype of Americans over age 65 is "poverty-stricken, sexless, isolated, lonely, unhappy, crippled

with disease, and dotty persons." When one recalls
that much of the past study of the aging person has
dealt with the problem of pathology and poverty, one
has an understanding of why a stereotype such as
this would be as widely accepted as it is.

Maggie Kuhn, founder of the Grey Panthers, an
activist group, sees five myths associated with old
age in America: it is a disease, is mindless, sexless,
useless, and powerless. When she observes that by
2000 AD (less than a quarter of a century away)
between one-third and one-fourth of the U.S. population will be over 65, one can readily see that we had
better examine our myths. We cannot afford to
believe that which is not so!

It is *not* a myth that what we are we are now becoming. Indeed, this is a sobering thought, but it can
be helpful to us in planning the direction of our own
lives if we remember that what older people are is re-
flected in the sum total of all their previous experiences. Again, we need to emphasize that the element of personal choice looms large in determining
the kind of person we are and are becoming. This is
not to over-emphasize that there are limits in terms of
our abilities but to emphasize that within the limita-
tions we have many important decisions to make
which vitally affect our own development.

In reviewing a number of myths, we shall be
looking at them under several categories: general considerations, living patterns, personal items, retirement, and death.

1. *General Considerations.* There are a number of
general myths abroad which do influence us. One is
that *aging is universally the same.* As a matter of
fact, the aging process is vastly different from person
to person. Overall, there are some general obser-

vations which one can make which are similar, but the outstanding difference is in the pace at which aging takes place in individuals. All of us have known some people who appear old at age 30 and others who appear young at age 80.

Unfortunately, many of us have a stereotyped concept of old people, with emphasis on the word "old." This leads us to the assumption that older people are different than other people. The cliches of "old man" and "old woman" blind us from seeing these people as significant individuals who may indeed be most remarkable individuals.

Another myth which is often accepted is that *life is all downhill,* particularly from the time of menopause. It has been discovered that people who come to life from the stance of flexibility are much more likely to see the joy and opportunity at each of life's phases, whether they are prior- or post-menopause experiences. Dr. Robert N. Butler, a prominent gerontologist of Washington, D.C. has explained that "our society has traditionally valued pragmatism, action, power, and the vigor of youth over contemplation, reflection, experience, and wisdom of age." It almost appears that the myths which we accept have been actively taught to us and that it is the exceptional person who sees these myths for what they are and does not allow himself to regard them as truths.

2. *Living Patterns.* It needs to be frankly stated that living patterns for aging people are different than living patterns for youth. But within this observation there are a number of considerations which are improperly interpreted. We shall refer to several. It is not true that *illness and old age are synonymous.* We now know that such things as living habits, diet, and exercise have a lot to do with health

at any age. Statistically, only about 13 percent of the people over age 65 experience a major limitation of their activity and only about 6 percent are housebound. We fall prey to the myth when we expect older people to be tottering and frail. Some older people respond to the expectation!

There is another myth which contends that *elderly people do not need as much food as younger people.* While mature adults require approximately 15 percent fewer calories than growing young people, one needs the same quantity of minerals and vitamins all through life and even more protein in the later years. A well-balanced diet is important at every age.

It is widely assumed that *older people prefer to live with their grown children.* This is a myth. Many of them do not wish to do so. They prefer independence and often remark that they would rather be free from the greater activity pattern of a younger household. This is not to say that elderly people want to be left alone, but it is to say that the living patterns have become more contemplative.

On the other hand, there are some who say that *older persons should not live alone.* However, approximately five million Americans over the age of 65 do live by themselves. This living alone may actually be harder on the children than on the parent. For those who prefer this pattern it is certainly an appropriate and constructive arrangement.

In our materialistic society, there continues a myth that *older people are expected to help their children.* The cliche, "I do not want my children to sacrifice as I sacrificed," may add to this expectation. However, more responsible reflection reveals the importance of individuals achieving for themselves versus having too much given to them.

A similar misconception is the idea that young people should be constantly kept around to help lift the morale of older persons. While this may be true for some older people, for others it definitely is not. Some older people prefer to live in a housing development restricted to persons of their own age!

In all these living patterns the individual differences stand out very markedly. In the study of myths this is the point that needs to be made over and over again.

3. *Personal Items.* A number of personal considerations which can be identified as myths need to be mentioned briefly. It is widely assumed that *intelligence reaches a peak about the age of 17 then declines throughout life* particularly so in later years. On the contrary, Dr. Carl Eistorfer, Director of the Gerontology Research Center at Duke University, indicates, " ... some of our recent work on blood pressure and intelligence has pretty well demonstrated that what a lot of people had accepted as a normal process of aging—the loss of intelligence between 65 and 75—is actually related to hypertension. In the group of subjects without hypertension, or where it was controlled, we see no intellectual drop."

Another personal myth which negatively affects elderly people is the widely held assumption that *late marriages are a mistake.* In truth, marriage at any age is a step which is serious and needs to be looked at in regard to the future and not only the present. The value of marriage lies in the complementary companionship two people give to each other, enabling each to live a more satisfactory life.

A study of 100 elderly couples who remarried after they were 65 reveals that three-fourths of the marriages were considered happy after a five-year period. A study likewise revealed that many of the grown children initially disapproved of their parent's remarriage, but 80 percent were favorable after the five-year period. Incidentally, many of the couples who remarried had been acquainted during their first marriages, having been neighbors or related through their first husbands or wives. The reasons advanced for remarriage were such considerations as the need to be needed, security, companionship, and sex.

An additional myth in American society is that *sexual activity is nonexistent or declines very sharply with age.* So much has been written in current society about sex that the question has in many circles grown all out of proportion. Nevertheless, we now have learned that we are basically sexual beings as long as we live. If we can accept this fact and shed off the baggage of ignorance we have displayed about it in the past, we will feel much better about our sexual identity throughout the entire aging process.

The "need to know" is not an age factor so much as a personal need. When this principle is applied to aging people at the point of their own physical changes or illness, it requires wisdom on the part of the doctor and the family to sense the quest of the older person for knowledge about himself/herself. This is a very important principle whether one is talking about physical ability, long-term illness, or impending surgery. Frequently, the anxiety of not knowing causes greater damage than the knowledge of what the current situation is. Many of us have resources of strength that come to the fore only when the facts of the situation are known.

4. *Retirement.* It would appear that we are making progress in our society toward understanding the

implications of retirement and the need to make preparations for it. *Retirement per se ought not be regarded as something which is dreaded* as less satisfying than life on the current scene. Conversation with people who are in the retirement years and who are enjoying the experience indicates that they are very busy people and have learned to fill their days with meaningful activity. There is a wealth of material available today on both the local and national levels which can be helpful in making personal preparations for the days of retirement. As we noted in the last chapter there is need for intentional communication between husband and wife to ascertain if their goals in retirement are as similar as they may assume them to be.

It should also be reiterated that retirement is a social adjustment for the wage earner who now needs to re-orient his daily schedule radically and who may no longer be in a position of being a desired person to whom many people gravitate because of his position. If the retiree is a husband he may need to guard against transferring his authority to his home. One couple faced precisely this problem. During the first months of his retirement, the husband stayed close to home and gave many suggestions to his wife concerning her need to be more efficient in caring for the household duties. Needless to say, she did not appreciate all these suggestions. The couple was wise enough to talk the matter through and discover that their happy marriage depended upon his finding interests outside of the home. This he did and it worked for the benefit of both partners.

When both husband and wife retire after sharing the "breadwinning" roles both may need to redirect their values and find new ways to creatively occupy their time. Both will discover the meaning of increased hours per day being spent together. Planning for retirement, therefore, should be a dual obligation of the husband-wife team.

Some persons tend to believe that retirement is a time to be spent reliving the past. To be sure, it is not part of a wholistic lifestyle to think only in the past. Older people have many experiences they delight in sharing. But the person who spends all his time reflecting on the past loses his orientation to the present and, it might be added, some of his popularity with his friends as well! But to reflect on the past thoughtfully, and to share as called upon, can be a very satisfying family experience. A notable example of this is the eagerness with which small grandchildren want to hear over and over again some of the stories from their grandparents' past.

Retirement thus brings with it many adjustments. The myths about which we have been reflecting together set forth the many challenging opportunities that come to the person who is willing to face the issues of his day. Life is uncertain at any age, but life can change quickly in advanced years. All of us know about the probabilities of ill health coming abruptly in the life of a person.

This leads us to another consideration: the possibility of institutional living. Statistically, only 1 percent of people age 65 and older are in a mental institution and less than 4 percent are in a home for the aging, nursing home, or penal institution. People of elderly years, therefore, do well to consider what they may need to do should they require the help of a home for the aged or a nursing home. There are people who are making a deliberate choice today because of the security which it offers for them.

Many fine retirement homes exist and with the increasing governmental regulations and the rising conscience of the church community, this trend should continue. This is a very hopeful contrast to the situation of a quarter century or more ago and reflects an option that is now available to more and more elderly people. Most persons make better choices when they consider options before the critical time for decision arrives.

On the other hand, the very fact that only 5 percent of people 65 years and older live in an institutional setting, does not excuse the remaining 95 percent from planning their retirement, nor should the church overlook these 95 percent who are members of the community around and the fellowship within the church. These people frequently need assistance in coping creatively with retirement.

One of the authors of this book received a long letter from his denominational headquarters indicating that he is at age 55 and will be receiving on a regular and periodic basis literature reminding him of the importance of making retirement plans now! In all honesty, the author had two reactions to receiving his mail which, incidentally, came unsolicited! His first reaction was, "I'm not old enough to make that kind of plan." But his second thought was one of gratitude, for while he and his wife have been doing some planning for retirement, it was good to know that the church is that much interested in what he will be doing as to help him to think creatively ten-fifteen years hence!

While the retirement age today is somewhat flexible, there are an increasing number of people in our society, including members of our congregations, who are in the retirement years of their lives. If the Gospel is meant for all expressions and all experiences of life, the church must provide education as part of its normal curriculum for life.

5. *Death.* A very destructive myth which continues with us and which may reflect our own reluctance to face the end of life is the *hesitancy and refusal of many persons to speak about death with older people.* In contrast to the popularly held belief that death talk is depressing to the elderly, many older people talk about death very matter-of-factly and with no morbidity at all. They recognize that chronologically their days are limited. All of us, in reflecting on our own attitudes toward death, will find that this affects our willingness to think about it with others. The older one becomes, the more likely he is to recognize that death is for him/her an impending fact. To be able to talk about it has many beneficial values and can affect positively the family plans for the future in carrying out the wishes of the older person who is needful of having this reflection and sharing it with loved ones.

Elisabeth Kubler-Ross has indicated that people who have been to the point of death and returned now have no fear of death. With the current interest in the questions of death and dying, we have more opportunity to talk both freely and frankly about one of the important issues which is part of all of us. Elsewhere in this book we will be dealing at greater length with this question.

Myths are ideas which deceptively take on the appearance of truths and gain sufficient momentum to achieve acceptance. The antidote is fact. Suggestions of this chapter are intended to open doors to more accurate understanding. When this is gained, the intent of the chapter will be realized.

Today well-lived ... makes every tomorrow a vision of Hope.—Anonymous

6
LIFE THROUGH
FAMILY LOVE

With the increasing number of people who are arriving to more advanced years than ever before, there are implications for the larger family unit. It has been said that "no man is an island unto himself" and this is certainly true for men and women of advanced years. In our society, and even in the church, too frequently these people have been relegated out-of-sight and out-of mind. Fortunately, both society and the church are beginning to show signs of recognizing this largest minority among us. The family too is challenged to give personal attention to the enrichment of the years of those who, by the grace of God, are able to live "three score and ten," and beyond.

The family is, and should be, involved in the aging experiences of the older person. As a matter of practical observation, it must be admitted that there are various degrees of this involvement, ranging all the way from neglect to making all the decisions for the older person!

We may well suspect that being involved in an intimate way and doing it with genuine empathy is extremely difficult for some of us because we have not yet had this experience for ourselves. On the other hand, as we grow through life we become increasingly aware of changes, such as the reduction of strength and speed. This awareness is helpful as a foundation upon which we can build to empathize with the person who is at the stage of life we have not yet experienced. It is difficult, but this is the challenge of life. Drawing a parallel from theology, it is not necessary to sin to be opposed to sinning. Likewise, it is not necessary to be old in order to be empathetically involved and concerned about the enrichment of life for those who have reached the later years of life.

The vast majority of people who come to the office of an administrator of a home for the aging to talk about the care of an aging person—whether it be a parent, a relative or a friend—come with some sense of guilt about what they are asking the home to do. Not many of those who come are seeking to escape responsibility, rather they feel the responsibility of either making or helping to make decisions which will result in better care and lifestyle for the aging person in the particular circumstance.

There are many problems involved, but these

problems may be seen as opportunities to share the Christian faith, to share the enrichment of life, and to actualize the concept that "no man is an island."

What are some of these problems?

1. *Living arrangements.* One obvious problem involved is that of living arrangements. A preacher was heard to say that the Christian answer to aging in the Scriptures is in three steps. The first choice of the aging person is to stay in his own home. The second choice is to live with his children. The third choice is to live in an institution, whether it is a retirement community or a nursing home. We would disagree with the categorizing of the biblical message in three different steps. Actually, *each* of these is an option for some people. For many people there are all three options, with variations. For some people, there may be only one, and it may be the institution, or it may be to live with the children, or it may be to stay in one's own home!

A family member needs to recognize and help the parent or grandparent to face honestly the options which are available. This may well be a slow process, but it is very important. As a matter of fact, these are questions we all will need to face in the future, and it is a part of wisdom to give attention to the matters ahead of time when, and if, it is possible.

For example, we all know that ours is an increasingly mobile society. Some parents have sold their properties upon retirement and have moved closer to their children only to have the son or son-in-law secure different employment and leave that community. Thus, the retired parents/grandparents who have placed "all their eggs in one basket" are now living in a strange community apart from their familiar patterns and apart from their families and friends.

If the choice of institutional life appears to be an option (and who knows for whom it may not be) with the increased possibility of illness for the older person, it is important to plan ahead. The plans may well need to be tentative. The procedure might be to schedule conversation with a home or homes which offer retirement and nursing care, to provide the opportunity for the aged person to visit and to talk with administrative personnel and with residents. It is helpful to be deliberate, to take time to plan well. It must be borne in mind that it is not possible to move into a good home on a day's notice!

2. *Health.* Fortunately, as we have seen, it is not true that old age and ill health are synonymous. However, it must be recognized that illness does come with increasing frequency to older people and that the recovery rate is slower than it had been in earlier life. The possibility of serious illness coming with little or no warning adds to the need of the aged and necessitates conversation with family members about some alternatives which may be utilized in the event that a crippling illness occurs.

3. *Financial considerations.* These are an increasingly difficult problem in an inflationary society. Persons who seek admission to a home for the aging often encounter the problem of inadequate finances. People in their 70's and 80's who apply for admission have accumulated what resources they have in a much different financial climate.

In addition, the forecast of the future calls for continuation of inflation. Some economists, who may be among the more hopeful, are saying that the rate of inflation will be reduced to 3 percent annually by 1990! So, if a person retires at 65 today on a fixed income, observe the financial problems which are inherent in living into the future.

Medical needs also require the family to see that there is adequate medical insurance to care for emergencies. Those who depend exclusively upon Medicare discover that there are a variety of items which are not covered. To make this discovery after the need has been experienced is often tragic.

Along with these financial considerations is the matter of estate planning for the future. It is important to have a will that one has designed with legal counsel. Everyone actually has a will whether he writes it or not because of the laws of the land. Christian stewardship does not end with the grave but actually ends when one's will is probated. A will should be made and then reviewed periodically as needs of the individual and the family change. It cannot be over-emphasized that reliable legal counseling and expertise are needed in the making or changing of a will to insure that one's wishes are carried out. We need not elaborate upon the observation that we are living in a changing society. Many of the values which were accepted without question in the past no longer seem to be so.

Many older people today are influenced heavily by the rural society in which they grew up and in which they lived most of their adult life, if not all of it. This was a different world than our present urban culture; even though we may live in the countryside, our lives are profoundly affected by what happens in the nation and in the world. Television has been both a positive and a negative influence, but no one can deny its transforming effect upon our perspective of the global community.

These changes lead to tensions because they represent different ways of looking at life. The older person has a different concept of leisure and often a different concept of the use of time. The present materialistic-minded society leads many of us to believe that we *buy* our recreation and our amusement. Those of advanced years frequently do not see it this way. In some issues moral values are involved, but in others the generational gap clearly produces tensions within the family.

4. *Understanding aging.* This leads us directly into a very important consideration: the importance of understanding the aging process. This can be enhanced by our very willingness to speak about it. How many people there are among us who are reluctant to share their birthdays, their age! How many among us refuse to talk about our own aging! Many children who counsel with an administrator about involving their aged parent in a home have extreme difficulty, primarily because they have not yet dealt with their *own* aging! It is not easy. It is most difficult to come to the realization that life has not only a beginning but an end. Fortunately, our society is starting to recognize the importance of teaching aging as inevitable and normal.

A recent study reported by Dr. Paul B. Baltes of Penn State University indicates that one's intellect does not need to decline with age. He says the question is not *whether* one can learn in older days, because one can. But the question is what does one want to learn and under what conditions will this learning take place? He reports two separate lines of research. The first has to do with relating chronological age to generational membership. He sees the older people at a disadvantage because of our better educational system today. (A minority of those today over 65 are high school graduates.) He also sees a shift in our educational programs within the past five years. With the increasing emphasis upon creativity, rather than physical prowess, there are expanding opportunities for the older person to be involved.

Increasingly, the medical profession is coming to understand that aging people should not be dismissed abruptly simply because they are 75 or 85. All of us can think of people of advanced years in our communities who were very ill but were fortunate enough to have a doctor who was committed to healing and did not dismiss the person because he or she was of advanced years.

We would hope that the medical profession will continue to grow in its ministry toward the aging. There is still no medical school in the nation that has a chair in gerontology. There are, however, educational centers across our nation which are working diligently at helping all of us understand how we age. With knowledge should come less fear.

5. *Decision making.* It is helpful to understand what we might call the "independence-dependence" syndrome. This is simply another way of saying that all of us need to maintain our independence as long as we can; and to recognize as well, that there have always been, and will continue to be, areas of our lives in which we are dependent upon one another. It is difficult to deal with one's parent or grandparent in making decisions of far reaching consequence, such as giving up a home and moving to an apartment, or moving to another residence, or living in with children and grandchildren. Just as difficult is the decision to go to an institution, a retirement community, or a nursing home. In the process of making this kind of decision, the person involved frequently fluctuates between declarations of independence, which

are sometimes very vigorously set forth, and saying,
"Do what is best," thus being very dependent.

The changing role/attitude of persons involved
in this process is difficult for the younger generation
to comprehend. Heretofore the parent/grandparent
had made his/her own decisions. Now suddenly the
decisions must be made by someone else! Frequently,
the child/grandchild is not thanked for taking this
interest and assuming this responsibility but may actually be severely criticized. It is worthwhile, at that
point, to be certain that, as one seeks to intellectualize the process, he or she sees the decision as having been made from an ethical base. It would be easy
at this point if we could simply say that this is the
answer, but that is not the way life is. We must sometimes sit back and intellectualize what we are doing
in order to accept it emotionally for ourselves.

6. *Dealing with death.* Again, one of the cruel
blows we often give to older people is to deny them
the opportunity to speak about their own death. Too
often we dismiss them by saying, "That's morbid,"
or, "That won't happen!" when we know, as a matter
of fact, it will. The older person is reassorting his
values and would like to have the opportunity frequently of talking of things which are important to
her/him. These frequently represent his/her life's
goals and achievements. These may deal with such
things as property, funeral service, many aspects of
the estate, or care for a companion who may survive.

7. *Communication.* The big word underlying
what we have been discussing in this chapter is communication. Communication is the ability and art of
speaking together. It is listening and hearing as well
as vocalizing. Communication is often lacking between generations in our society, but with mutual ef-

fort this need not be so.

8. *The church.* We are blessed today with an increasing number of pastors and lay people in our churches who are concerned about the family's involvement in the aging process. Some pastors have classes which deal with these issues, involving the largest minority in our congregations and society.

The greatest contribution the church can make is to provide ongoing opportunities within the fellowship for intergenerational experiences. In the past we have strictly divided our educational program by age groupings. We are coming to recognize that while these age groupings continue to have some value they are not to be viewed exclusively. Much valuable experience has been gained by groups within the congregation meeting across age lines and sharing together creatively on the issues and interests of life. It resembles the values of the households of the past. The church can provide an opportunity for the young to learn from the old and the old to experience the pleasures of associating with and learning from the young. To include this kind of approach as the normal pattern of experience, a model of which is our Sunday morning worship service, is to attest to the fact that within our community there is this diversity of age. This is as it should be. God has not intended us to isolate ourselves from one another. Rather, God intends us to be together, in community.

A member of a family that has living relatives spanning four generations has a unique and educational opportunity to study and identify with the aging process. The church has a similar opportunity to bring people of all ages together.

The intergenerational approach sounds rather pompous and complicated, but it actually means accepting and taking life as it is and using this as the fabric and the curriculum for teaching the involvement of the family in the process of aging. The approach will enable us to have some expertise as we seek to deal with one important aspect of the aging process, helping the aged person to make the best decision about lifestyle in the last days of his or her life on this earth.

The Bible speaks frequently about the virtues of age. To be able to tap the spiritual heritage of the past and add to it the increasing knowledge of the present can be helpful to us in our own family situations in the immediate and far future.

"For I know the plans I have for you, says the Lord. They are plans for good, not for evil, to give you a future and a hope." Jeremiah 29:11.

Shuffle-Shoon and Amber-Locks
Sit together, building blocks;
Shuffle-Shoon is old and grey,
Amber-Locks a little child.
But together at their play
Age and Youth are reconciled.
              —Eugene Field (1850-1895)

May the God of hope fill you with all joy and peace in believing, so that by the power of the Holy Spirit you may abound in hope. —Romans 15:13

7
CONFIDENCE IN THE FACE OF DEATH

Charlie was a kind gentleman who exhibited a sense of warmth and openness. In his 80 years of living he sought to approach life with understanding and sensitivity. He usually succeeded. But on this day things were different. He felt uptight and unnerved. As he stood gazing toward the second floor of the nursing home, tears began to stream down his cheeks. He felt all choked up inside. At that moment a friend, passing by on the sidewalk, stopped to chat. Noticing Charlie's apparent stress, the friend inquired of his dilemma.

Being scarcely able to talk for the emotional tor-

ment, Charlie pointed to the nursing wing of the
home and blurted out these words,

"I don't want to go there! I'm not afraid to die,
but I don't want to have to go through all the agony
of dying."

Charlie's problem is not unique to him. The fear
of dying is a major reason why people do not want to
talk about aging or death. Despite the fact that books
are being written which analyze the stages of death,
and aside from the fact that the Christian faith
teaches the hope of life beyond death, people still
resist the process of dying.

Part of the stigma attached to death and dying
comes from our culture's view of life which is primarily materialistic. We are taught from the time that we
are children that our living should be comprised of
doing only those things which make us happy and
bring to us feelings of success and enjoyment. And, of
course, the "things" which bring us all of these are
materialistic products. Is it any wonder that families
or individuals so attached to this "success" oriented
lifestyle will have fears about the process which
brings an end to life?

But there is also a theological side to how one un-
derstands death. To be sure, the process of dying is
not pleasant. There is often pain, emotional stress,
problems of communication, and a sense of extreme
loneliness. One elderly lady put it this way:

"Sometimes I wonder if God really loves me any-
more, because I can't do the things I did all my life
and I don't look as nice as I used to."

In contrast to this person's understanding of
God's love was another lady who, facing the agony
and torment of heart failure and arteriosclerosis,
called upon the nursing home chaplain to come and

pray with her. She said,

"I just want to let God completely take over my life."

Having said that, she quietly and calmly slept away as the chaplain repeated Psalm 23 and had prayer.

Each of these approached death with a different viewpoint and expectation about life, God, individual identity, and self-worth. While the first person understood God's love as dependent upon her ability to perform, the second person found peace in God's acceptance of her as she was. For her, "just to be," at that point in her life, was a blessing.

How we see our life and the opportunity for creative Christian living may, in part, determine how we see our own aging and death. The whole view of death in the New Testament is a process with suffering, pain, and separation to be sure. But it is also a release and a time of quietness and rest which has, in Christ, the promise of eternal and renewed life.

Many times families have failed to take into account the fact that life in our materialistic culture is not forever. As a result, they face fear, sadness, and separation when a loved one dies. Though many families shudder at the thought, there is nothing wrong with planning one's funeral.

At the appropriate time parents should sit down with their children and talk about the eventuality of their death, what this means, and how they would like their Christian funeral to be conducted. If it is important to see one's death in the context of Christian life, then a Christian funeral should be a time of worship and celebration of God's love and care for his people. Open caskets, viewing dead bodies, and a sense of morbidity can be offset and even replaced by hymns of strength, litanies which deal with life, and sermons which deal with the understanding of the life cycle and death. If families could sit down together and plan for death from this perspective, there would be less chance of funerals becoming expensive because of the need for a lavish emotional release from the fear of one's own dying.

Recently a pastor had the misfortune of having both of his elderly parents die within a month of each other. He relates how he and his brothers made the coffin, dug the grave, and planned the worship service. Rather than being a morbid experience, the working out of preparations became a catharsis for the process of grief which usually accompanies death.

Not everyone is equipped emotionally to handle death as did this pastor and his family, but every family can begin by talking about and planning for the eventuality of death and a Christian funeral service to follow. This is not to say that such discussions will be free of anxiety, but it is to suggest that a more healthy climate of acceptance can be created when the family shares fears, feelings, and hopes about death.

It is precisely at this point where the church can provide a nurturing influence upon the attitudes of its members regarding aging and death. Some congregations have begun to plan intergenerational classes in their church schools, as well as providing opportunities during the week for several family clusters (by geographical areas) to gather for study and fellowship.

In these settings positive role models are being provided for young and old to experience the thoughts, feelings and behavior patterns of each other. As this happens, young people discover that being old is not a dreaded stigma, and older people discover that young people have an acceptance of the older people which is strengthening for their own lives.

As the above suggested models reveal, the church can play an important role in building a positive image of the process of aging. There are activities which the local congregation can provide which are meaningful opportunities for people to consider the subject of death and dying.

Several years ago a young pastor and his wife were encouraged to attend a Wills Emphasis Workshop sponsored by their denominational judicatory. In the midst of the discussion, both husband and wife came to a new realization that their lives, their possessions, and their relationship were only for a season when viewed against the panorama of time as God, the Creator, had planned it. A new understanding of aging and death was caught by the pair as they evaluated their possessions and their own lives. The couple realized that their regard for "things" needed to be reviewed against the totality of the creation itself.

Until that workshop the couple never thought of dying. Since they were in good health and enjoying life, these two had viewed death as a far removed possibility of existence. Yet, as they began to hear ideas about planning for death by making a "living" will, the idea of mortality and separation became more real, whereas, before the workshop the ideas of growing old were just never even considered. Suddenly, the couple began to see aging and death as natural and expected parts of the life process.

The startling fact for them was not only the realization of their own mortality, but coming to

know that the state would dictate the disposition of
their assets and estate if they died without a will. To
ignore planning for their death, they discovered,
would impose a hardship on their children and family.

The church and its related institutions offer to
people an excellent opportunity for Christian
stewardship in regard to possessions beyond the immediate members of the family. Too often people fail
to plan for proper distribution of their estates because
they are afraid to speak or even think about their
own deaths.

Just as important as birth is to a Christian family, so is the experience of death. Though each person
and family will have anxieties and certain fears
about death, the process is a part of our total life cycle. These fears and apprehensions can be a part of
our being on the growing edge of life, or they can
create an inner anxiety which many people carry
needlessly to their graves.

A model that congregations are using consists of
study courses on death and dying. Recently, a middle
aged woman confided to her pastor that, as a result of
a study group on the subject of death, her husband
came to accept the death of his father. For eleven
years until that study group, he had been unable to
even talk about his father's death. For the first time,
he was freed from fear, anxiety, and grief over the
loss of his father. He could now accept his father's
death and began to see the reality of his own aging
and death.

A realization that life is not dependent upon
culture or material values moves us to an awareness
that we need to consider and plan for the experience
of dying. To do so is an affirmation of our faith in

Christ, who brings life even in the midst of death.

Hope is the last thing that dies in man, and
although it be exceedingly deceitful, yet it is of this
good use to us, that while we are traveling through life
it conducts us in an easier and more pleasant way to
our journey's end.
          —Francois de la Rochefoucauld (1613-1680)

AS I GROW OLD
God keep my heart attuned to laughter
When youth is done;
When all the days are gray days, coming after
The warmth, the sun.
God keep me then from bitterness, from grieving,
When life seems cold.
God keep me always loving and believing
As I grow old.

—Author unknown

BIBLIOGRAPHY

Abernathy, Jean B., Old is Not a Four Letter Word. Abingdon Press, Nashville, 1975.

Aisquith, Glenn H., Living Creatively as an Older Adult. Herald Press, Scottsdale, 1975.

Brown, J. Paul, Counseling With Senior Citizens. Fortress Press, Philadelphia, 1968.

Butler, Robert N., M.D., Why Survive? Being Old in America. Harper & Row, New York, 1975.

Clingan, Donald F., Aging Persons in the Community of Faith. Indiana Commission on the Aging and Aged. 1975.

Fritz, Dorothy Bertolet, Growing Old is a Family Affair. John Knox Press, Richmond, 1972.

Howe, Reuel L., The Creative Years. Seabury Press, New York, 1959.

——————————, How to Stay Younger While Growing Older. Wonder Books, Waco, 1974.

Kubler-Ross, Elisabeth, Death—the Final Stage of Growth. Prentice-Hall, New Jersey, 1975.

——————————, On Death and Dying. Macmillan Co., New York, 1969.

Mow, Anna B., So Who's Afraid of Birthdays? Lippincott Co., New York, 1969.

National Council on the Aging, Inc., The Myth and Reality of Aging in America. Louis Harris and Associates, 1975.

Nouwen, Henri J. M. and Walter J. Gaffney, Aging, the Fulfillment of Life. Doubleday, Garden City, 1974.

Percy, Charles H., Growing Old in the Country of the Young. *McGraw-Hill, New York, 1974.*

Rommel, Kurt, The Best Is Yet To Be. *Fortress Press, Philadelphia, 1975.*

Rosamonde, R. Boyd and Charles G. Oakes, ed., Foundations of Practical Gerontology, *University of South Carolina, 1973.*

Scherzer, Carl J., Ministering to the Dying. *Fortress Press, Philadelphia, 1969.*

Westberg, Granger E., Good Grief. *Fortress Press, Philadelphia, 1962.*

Wolff, Hans Walter, Anthropology of the Old Testament. *Fortress Press, Philadelphia, 1974.*

FOURTEEN QUESTIONS TO ASK
OF YOUR CONGREGATION REGARDING
MINISTRY TO/WITH/FOR AGING PEOPLE

1. *What is your congregation doing about the feelings of loneliness experienced by elderly people?*

2. *Is your church building constructed to accommodate elderly people? If not, what can be done about it?*

3. *Is there a need for transportation of elderly people to church or for other services?*

4. *Do elderly people stay away from being involved in the church? If so, why?*

5. *What is needed to involve more elderly people in your fellowship?*

6. *Can your congregation provide a needed ministry to/with aging people through cooperating with an area agency on aging?*

7. *Are elderly people represented on the church board or other decision making bodies of the church?*

8. *Is there a balance of programming for all age groups in your church?*

9. *Do you remember widows, widowers, and single people as you build your congregational programming?*

10. *Are there opportunities in your congregation for intergenerational exchange and fellowship gatherings for discussion of ideas?*

11. *Has your congregation explored social action kinds of ministry involving aging people (e.g. visiting shut-ins, daily telephoning and/or a meal program)?*

12. *Could there be a day care program for senior citizens established in your church?*

13. *Are bulletins and newsletters printed in large type so as to be read easily by elderly members?*

14. *Can elderly people hear adequately in the church facilities?*